G

CENGAGE Learning

Drama for Students, Volume 1

Staff

David Galens and Lynn M. Spampinato, *Editors*

Thomas Allbaugh, Craig Bentley, Terry Browne, Christopher Busiel, Stephen Coy, L. M. Domina, John Fiero, Carol L. Hamilton, Erika Kreger, Jennifer Lewin, Sheri Metzger, Daniel Moran, Terry Nienhuis, Bonnie Russell, Arnold Schmidt, William Wiles, Joanne Woolway, *Contributing Writers*

Elizabeth Cranston, Kathleen J. Edgar, Joshua Kondek, Marie Lazzari, Tom Ligotti, Marie Napierkowski, Scot Peacock, Mary Ruby, Diane Telgen, Patti Tippett, Kathleen Wilson, Pam Zuber, *Contributing Editors*

Pamela Wilwerth Aue, *Managing Editor*

Jeffery Chapman, *Programmer/Analyst*

Victoria B. Cariappa, *Research Team Manager*
Michele P. LaMeau, Andy Guy Malonis, Barb

McNeil, Gary Oudersluys, Maureen Richards, *Research Specialists*

Julia C. Daniel, Tamara C. Nott, Tracie A. Richardson, Cheryl L. Warnock, *Research Associates*

Susan M. Trosky, *Permissions Manager*
Kimberly F. Smilay, *Permissions Specialist*
Sarah Chesney, *Permissions Associate*
Steve Cusack, Kelly A. Quin, *Permissions Assistants*

Mary Beth Trimper, *Production Director*
Evi Seoud, *Assistant Production Manager*
Shanna Heilveil, *Production Assistant*

Randy Bassett, *Image Database Supervisor*
Mikal Ansari, Robert Duncan, *Imaging Specialists*
Pamela A. Reed, *Photography Coordinator*

Cynthia Baldwin, *Product Design Manager*
Cover design: Michelle DiMercurio, *Art Director*
Page design: Pamela A. E. Galbreath, *Senior Art Director*

ISSN applied for and pending

Printed in the United States of America
10 9 8 7 6 5 4 3

The Glass Menagerie

Tennessee Williams

1944

Introduction

The Glass Menagerie was originally produced in Chicago in 1944 and then staged in New York on Broadway in 1945. The text was also published in 1945. This play was the first of Williams's to win the New York Drama Critics Circle Award, an honor he was given four times. Although *The Glass Menagerie* also received much popular acclaim, some critics believe that the thematic devices that Williams relies on, such as the legends on the screen, are too heavy-handed.

The Glass Menagerie is autobiographical in its sources. In some ways, this is a coming of age story, with both Tom Wingfield and Laura Wingfield negotiating their roles as young adults. Like many coming of age stories, the major conflicts in this play are both internal and external; Tom cannot choose both the future he desires for himself and the future his mother, Amanda Wingfield, desires for him and for Laura. Emerging through this major conflict between Tom and Amanda are the themes of alienation and loneliness, duty and responsibility, and appearances and reality.

Through its poetic structure and reliance on stage technology, *The Glass Menagerie* has had a significant impact on later twentieth century drama. Tom serves as both narrator and character, dissolving the present into the past; Williams signals this by exploiting lighting and sound, especially music—technologies which were less available to earlier playwrights. In this sense, the themes of the play are inseparable from its production values.

Author Biography

Tennessee Williams was born in Mississippi in 1911. His given name was Thomas Lanier Williams. His family lived in Mississippi and Tennessee until 1918, when they moved to St. Louis, Missouri, where Williams's father, Cornelius, worked as a shoe salesman. This move to a metropolitan area was difficult for both Williams and his sister, Rose. Williams's family was Episcopalian and his grandfather a minister, although Williams himself converted to Roman Catholicism in 1969. As an adult, he moved frequently, living in such cities as St. Louis and New York. Many critics base their interpretation of *The Glass Menagerie* as autobiographical in part because of the similarities between the Wingfield family and Williams's own. Williams's mother, Edwina, was a Southern belle, and his older sister, Rose, to whom Williams was close, suffered from schizophrenia as an adult.

Williams attended the University of Missouri from 1931 until 1933 and Washington University in St. Louis from 1936 until 1937 before earning his A.B. degree from the University of Iowa in 1938. He began publishing his work in magazines when he was only twelve years old and decided to become a playwright at the age of twenty, although he also wrote short stories, poems, novels, and memoirs. As a young man, he supported himself with various jobs, including waiter, teletype operator, and theater usher.

After *The Glass Menagerie* was produced on Broadway in 1945, however, Williams consistently had his new work produced in various New York theaters, often averaging one play every other year. He was not only prolific but also successful. His plays won many honors, beginning with the Group Theatre Award in 1939. This was followed by a Rockefeller Foundation fellowship. He won the New York Drama Critics Circle Award four times, and he won the Pulitizer Prize for *A Streetcar Named Desire,* his other most well-known play, in 1948. Williams was the first recipient of the centennial medal from New York's Episcopal Cathedral of St. John the Divine in 1973. During the last decade of his life, he received a Kennedy Honors Award and was elected to the Theatre Hall of Fame.

Williams's most popular plays were also produced as movies, and he frequently served as screenwriter, sometimes with a collaborator. His later work continues the themes of his early plays, and he is sometimes accused of failing to develop further. In part because of this, his audience began to drift away near the end of his life.

Tennessee Williams died by choking in a hotel in New York City in 1983.

Plot Summary

Scene I

    The Glass Menagerie opens with some fairly elaborate stage directions which serve both to describe the setting and to introduce themes and symbols through their tone. For example, the apartments in the Wingfields' neighborhood are described as "warty growths" and the people as "one interfused mass of automatism." Tom Wingfield is the first character on stage, and he functions here as both narrator and interpreter. In this role, Tom exists several years after the primary action of the play. He introduces the other characters, and his presence in this role guides the audience in the direction of the play.

memory play.

    The action begins with Amanda, Tom's mother, calling him to the supper table. Throughout the meal, Amanda instructs and criticizes Tom in his eating habits, until Tom responds with disgust. At once, the audience realizes that Tom and Amanda live in a state of tension. The other character present at this meal is Laura, Tom's sister, who wears a brace on her leg. When Laura offers to serve the dessert, Amanda says that she wishes Laura to "stay fresh and pretty—for gentlemen callers!" Amanda will remain concerned with the possibility of "gentlemen callers" for Laura throughout the play, and here she reminisces about her own youthful days. When Laura indicates that she's not expecting any gentlemen callers, Amanda appears to be astonished, although this conversation seems to be a frequent one. Laura explains that "I'm not popular like you [Amanda] were."

Scene II

As this scene begins, Laura is sitting alone in the living room, washing the animals in her glass collection. Amanda enters, clearly upset. Their conversation reveals that although Laura has been enrolled in a typing course, and although she has left the apartment every day as if to attend her class, she has in fact not been going. Amanda had stopped by to speak with Laura's teacher, who revealed that Laura had become ill during a typing test and had not returned. Laura admits that she simply goes to the zoo nearly every day.

Amanda is concerned about Laura's future because she has no prospective husband, nor does she have any skills by which she could make a living. Laura says that she had like a boy once, while she was in high school, although she is now twenty-three years old. This boy's name was Jim, and he was very popular then and predicted to be very successful. Jim had called Laura by the nickname "Blue Roses" because he had misunderstood her when she had said she'd been sick with pleurosis.

Scene III

This scene opens with Tom again functioning as narrator and describing the changes that occurred in the family over the next several weeks. Amanda became even more concerned with "gentlemen callers." Because she believes that the apartment will have to be redecorated if gentlemen callers begin to arrive, she takes a job selling magazine subscriptions.

The major portion of this scene consists of an argument between Tom and Amanda. Amanda has thrown away some of Tom's books because they were written by D. H. Lawrence, a British writer some people considered scandalous. The argument continues when Tom says he is going out to the movies, although Amanda replies that no one can go to as many movies as Tom claims to. She implies that Tom is lying, especially since he often comes home late and apparently drunk. She is worried that he will lose his job because he so frequently goes to work when he has had only three or four hours of sleep. She urges him to think of the good of the family rather than only himself. Tom replies by emphasizing how much he hates his job and slams out of the apartment after calling Amanda an "ugly—babbling old—witch."

Scene IV

Tom arrives home much later. Laura lets him in, apparently believing that he really has been to the movies. Laura asks Tom to apologize to Amanda at breakfast, which he eventually does.

does not use
the conflict

Amanda sends Laura out to buy some butter so that she can have a few words alone with Tom. She explains that she is worried that Tom is becoming like his father, who had abandoned the family. Amanda assures Tom that he will be able to go wherever and do whatever he wants as soon as Laura is secure in a future. She asks Tom to bring home an acquaintance from the warehouse where he works to meet Laura, though Tom does not respond enthusiastically to the prospect.

Slightly foreboding?

Scene V

You can see Amanda does really care here.

Tom and Amanda argue about whether he smokes too much. Eventually, Tom reveals that he has invited someone home to dinner, and that he's coming tomorrow. Amanda panics because of all of the preparations that will have to be made. Tom says that the man's name is James Delaney O'Connor and that he works as a shipping clerk, making approximately eighty-five dollars per month (Tom makes sixty-five dollars per month). Tom urges Amanda not to anticipate too much, since Laura is "crippled," a word she reprimands him for using, and "peculiar." The scene ends with Tom once again leaving for the movies.

Scene VI

The scene begins with Amanda and Laura preparing supper. Laura is extremely nervous and becomes even more upset when she discovers that the visitor's name is Jim O'Connor, since that was the name of the boy she liked in high school. Tom and Jim arrive, and Jim discusses his future he hopes for in public speaking. Tom reveals that he has joined The Union of Merchant Seamen and has paid his dues with the money he was supposed to use for the electric bill. Amanda enters wearing an old dress from her youth and acting extremely coy. Amanda claims that Laura has prepared the supper, but when it is time to eat, Laura is so nervous that she becomes ill. She rests on the sofa throughout dinner.

Scene VII

As Tom, Amanda, and Jim are eating, the lights go out. Amanda assumes they have blown a fuse, though Jim says none of the fuses look faulty. Amanda urges Jim to keep Laura company in the living room. Laura reveals that she had known Jim in high school, and he eventually remembers who she is. She says that she had always felt conspicuous because of her brace, but Jim assures her that it was hardly noticeable. Laura has kept a program from a play Jim had starred in, and he autographs it for her. He reveals that he broke up with his high school girlfriend. When he asks Laura what she has done since high school, she states that her glass collection keeps her very busy.

Jim suggests that she simply needs more self confidence and begins talking about inferiority complexes. Laura shows him her favorite glass animal, a unicorn. Because music is audible from the dance hall across the alley, Jim asks Laura to dance. While they dance, they bump the table; the unicorn falls off and breaks its horn, though Laura says now he's like the other horses rather than being "feakish." Telling Laura that she is pretty, Jim kisses her. A few minutes later, though, he confesses that he is engaged, and that he hadn't realized Tom had invited him home in order to meet Laura. She gives him the broken unicorn. Amanda serves lemonade, and Jim tells her also that he is engaged. Embarrassed, Amanda assumes that Tom had been playing a mean-spirited joke on them. Tom leaves again, though this time his departure is permanent. The play concludes with Laura blowing out the candles.

Characters

Blue Roses

See Laura Wingfield

Jim O'Connor

Jim is the gentleman caller Tom invites home for dinner. Although he also works at the warehouse, he makes more money than Tom and has greater aspirations—even if they are somewhat conventional ones. Yet, his situation reveals that dreams are often not achieved, for in high school Jim had been predicted to become very successful. He treats Laura kindly, but during their conversation he reveals that he too is not entirely realistic, for he discounts the severity of Laura's problem and assures her that all she needs is more confidence.

Amanda Wingfield

Amanda is the mother of Tom and Laura. She has difficulty facing reality, though by the end of the play she does acknowledge Tom's desire to leave and Laura's uncertain future. She frequently fantacizes about the past, probably exaggerating her own popularity then. Her relationship with Tom is conflicted, most prominently when she criticizes his minor habits.

Laura Wingfield

Laura is the daughter of Amanda and sister of Tom. She is extremely shy, even emotionally disturbed, and she wears a brace on her leg which makes her feel conspicuous. Her collection of glass animals gives the play its title. She does not work, and she has been unable to complete a typing class because of her nervousness. Although she says she had once liked a boy in high school, she has never had and is unlikely to have any kind of romantic relationship.

Tom Wingfield

Amanda's son and Laura's brother, Tom is the protagonist of the play. He dreams of abandoning the family, as his father had done. He feels trapped in his job, where he often neglects his duties in order to write poetry, and in his home, where he is reprimanded for reading some modern literature which was considered scandalous at the time. Although he claims to go to the movies every night, he also probably goes to a bar, since he sometimes comes home drunk. Eventually, he agrees to bring a "gentleman caller" home to meet Laura, but he leaves the family that night. Although Tom appears to genuinely care for Laura, his greater desire is to relieve his frustration at his confining situation. When he functions as narrator at a time several years after the action of the play, readers understand that he has escaped physically but not emotionally.

Themes

Appearances and Reality

Throughout this play, emerging in every scene and through the actions of every character is the theme of Appearances vs. Reality. Characters believe in a future and a past which are not realistic, and these beliefs affect the decisions they make regarding their relationships with each other. For example, Amanda frequently describes the days of her youth, when she claims she received "seventeen!—gentlemen callers!" during one Sunday afternoon. Although she describes these men as if they either are wealthy or have died a tragic/heroic death, the man she married was apparently both unsuccessful and irresponsible. And despite all evidence to the contrary, Amanda seems to believe that Laura, too, will one day be visited by similar gentlemen callers.

Media Adaptations

- *The Glass Menagerie* was released as a film by Warner Brothers in 1950. This black and white version was produced by Jerry Wald and Charles K. Feldman and directed by Irving Rapper. It starred Jane Wyman as Laura Wingfield, Kirk Douglas as Jim O'Connor, Gertrude Lawrence as Amanda Wingfield, and Arthur Kennedy as Tom Wingfield. It also included roles for several characters who are only referred to in the play.

- Another version of *The Glass Menagerie* was filmed by Cineplex Odeon and released in 1987. It was produced by Burtt Harris and directed by Paul Newman.

Newman's wife, Joanne Woodward played Amanda; John Malkovich played Tom; Karen Allen played Laura; and James Naughton played the gentleman caller. It is available on video through MCA/Universal Home Video.

- A television adaptation also aired on CBS in 1966. This version starred Shirley Booth as Amanda, Hal Holbrook as Tom, Barbara Loden as Laura, and Pat Hingle as Jim. David Susskind was the producer and Michael Elliott the director.

- Another television version was broadcast on ABC in 1984.

- A sound recording has also been produced by Caedmon. This two-cassette version was released in 1973; the cast consists of Montgomery Clift, Julie Harris, Jessica Tandy, and David Wayne.

Rather than fantasizing about his past, Tom believes that his future holds excitement, if he can only escape his family. Yet he fails to escape completely even though he does leave. In his last monologue, Tom reveals that he is not running toward something but away from his past: "I was pursued by something." And although he travels continually, he fails to find the excitement he longs for, as the "cities swept about me like dead leaves."

Even Jim O'Connor, the most conventional character, continues to believe in unattainable dreams. Although he apparently is talented, he has been unable to make choices that will guarantee him professional success. He refers enthusiastically to his public speaking class, but readers understand that Jim is attributing more significance to this course than it perhaps deserves.

Laura, however, is the character who is most obviously detached from reality. She cannot have normal interactions with other people without becoming ill. Her emotional energy is invested in her collection of glass animals, which may be exotic and delicate but are nevertheless "unreal," especially the unicorn she claims is her favorite. For the unicorn doesn't even represent a realistic animal. Even the nickname Jim once gave her, Blue Roses, is a flower that doesn't exist. By the time the play ends, Laura seems to be more detached from reality rather than able to adjust.

Coming of Age

Although most pieces of literature which have "coming of age" as a major theme discuss younger characters, in some ways *The Glass Menagerie* also considers this theme. While all of the characters are technically adults, they do not relate to each other as adults. Amanda instructs Tom about his eati-- habits as if he is still a child, and he re-- with the resentment of an adolescent. In.

Tom is in a double bind, for he cannot simultaneously exercise all of the qualities of an adult in his situation. If he is to fulfill his family obligations, obligations Amanda has thrust upon him rather than ones which he has voluntarily assumed, he will have to relinquish his independence. If he is to act independently, he will have to forsake his family responsibilities. Although Tom does eventually assert his independence, he does not seem to ever become fully mature. Rather, he is compared to his father, who also abandoned the family, though he had presumably chosen that responsibility by getting married. It is his father's desertion which places Tom into such an oppressive situation. Because Tom is so clearly compared to his father, readers can easily forget this primary difference between them.

Topics for Further Study

- Although *The Glass Menagerie* is

set in the 1930s, many critics describe it as timeless. Describe the historical changes you would have to make if you were to set the play today.

- Research the financial situation of single mothers today and compare their options to those of Amanda.

- Examine the catalogs of several business or technical schools in your area and compare their curricula to the apparent curriculum of Rubicam's Business College, where Laura has been attending typing classes.

- Interview someone in your school who has worked on the production of a play. Focus your questions especially on the technical aspects of stage craft so that you can discover how the screens, lighting, *etc.* would work in *The Glass Menagerie*.

Duty and Responsibility

Woven into the coming of age theme is the issue of duty and responsibility. While Amanda insists that Tom's primary duty is to her and Laura, Tom resents this responsibility because it presents him with so few options. On the other hand, Tom also has a responsibility to himself, one he might say he exercises precisely by attempting to abandon his family. By the end of the play, however, we see that Tom is both irresponsible and a failure in attaining his goals. Yet, the responsibilities of a son are different from those of a father. Although Amanda, in some ways, wants Tom to be a surrogate husband—she holds him responsible for supporting the family although she does not permit him the authority of a head of a household—Tom's action, while being objectively similar to his father's, might not be identical morally.

Style

Conflict

Although the action in *The Glass Menagerie* occurs over only a couple of days, nearly every scene is laden with overt conflict. The most obvious conflict occurs between Tom and Amanda, since Tom needs to remove himself from the family in order to achieve his goals, while Amanda needs him to stay. This conflict is most evident during their frequent bickering about the way Tom chews his food or the number of cigarettes he smokes. A more significant conflict, however, occurs within Tom's character. In order to follow his dream, vague as it is, he will have to abandon not only Amanda but also Laura.

Narrator

Although most plays do not rely on a narrator, *The Glass Menagerie* is structured so that Tom can fulfill two roles. He is both a character in the play and the person who, at times, tells the story directly to the audience. This occurs particularly at the beginning of the play, when Tom summarizes the events that have preceded the action and describes the setting, and at the end of the play, when Tom reveals what has happened to him during the intervening years.

Protagonist

The protagonist of a literary work is the main character, who must change in some way during the course of the events, even if the change is entirely internal. Tom is clearly the protagonist of *The Glass Menagerie*. Although he is not heroic and will probably never triumph over his obstacles, he does take action by the end of the play.

Setting

The broad setting of *The Glass Menagerie*—as described in Williams's stage directions—is "one of those vast hive-like conglomerations of cellular living-units that flower as warty growths in overcrowded urban centers of lower middle-class population." In other words, it is a fairly large apartment house in a comparatively poor neighborhood. The specific city is unnamed, as if details are unnecessary since these neighborhoods so closely resemble each other. All of the action occurs within the living room and dining room of the Wingfield's apartment; the primary importance of the setting is to reinforce the cramped feeling the characters struggle against. The time is also vague. Obviously, the play is set several decades ago, since Tom can support (although inadequately) a family of three on sixty-five dollars a month; yet, were it not for details such as these, the play could easily be set in the current generation.

Symbolism

The Glass Menagerie achieves part of its effect through the prominent display of symbols. The father's portrait looms above the family on their wall, although he has been absent for years; obviously, he remains psychologically present and significantly affects the attitudes of the other characters. The candles also function symbolically. When Tom fails to pay the light bill, Amanda lights the apartment with candles, suggesting that this will lend a more romantic atmosphere to their home. The last action of the play is when Laura blows the candles out, as if this will erase her from Tom's memory in a death-like moment.

The primary symbol in this play, however, is Laura's glass menagerie, particularly the unicorn. The glass animals are fragile, as Laura is both emotionally and physically. Although they might imitate reality, they are not in themselves real, and their primary value lies in Laura's imagination. When the unicorn's horn breaks off, Laura describes him as now like the other horses, as if one must be broken in order to be normal. Laura is already "broken," however, and has never had the mythic status of a unicorn; she will never attain normalcy.

Historical Context

World War II

Although the setting of *The Glass Menagerie* is the 1930s, during the Great Depression and slightly before the beginning of World War II, Williams wrote the play after America had entered the war but before a decisive victory had been achieved. After being produced in Chicago in 1944, the play arrived in New York in 1945, the year the war ended. For Americans, the most significant historical event of the first half of the 1940s was the entry of the United States into World War II. Although the United States had not been eager to enter this war, Japan bombed Pearl Harbor on December 7, 1941, making U.S. participation inevitable on the side of the Allies—primarily England, France, and Russia. In addition to Japan, the Allies fought against Germany, led by Adolf Hitler, and Italy, led by Benito Mussolini. Through most of the war, Franklin Roosevelt was President of the United States, until he died on April 12, 1945; he was succeeded by his vice president, Harry S. Truman. The European phase of the war ended in May 1945, and the Pacific phase ended with the dropping of nuclear bombs on Japan (in Hiroshima and Nagasaki) in August of 1945.

Women in the Workforce

Among the American ramifications of World War II was the sudden increase of women in the workplace. Primarily because so many men were serving in the armed forces, women began performing jobs that had not previously been open to them, in factories for example; such work was now considered patriotic. "Rosy the Riveter" is a famous character who represents this trend. When the war ended and men returned home, however, women were expected to leave their jobs so that the men might find employment. Women did not enter the workforce in significant numbers again until the 1970's.

Compare & Contrast

- **1930s:** Adolf Hitler begins to achieve power in Germany. Some Americans fought in the Spanish Civil War, although the United States did not officially participate. World War II began in Europe in 1939, but the United States declared its neutrality.

  1940s: During World War II, most men served in the military, unless they were exempt for health or other reasons. Because so many people were affected, this war received prominent attention both in politics and in individual daily lives.

  Today: Although The United States

has engaged in comparatively minor military engagements during the last generation, no given war has become a cultural obsession since the Vietnam War ended in the mid-1970s. While men must register for the draft when they reach the age of 18, no one is currently drafted, and the military consistently speaks of "down sizing."

- **1930s:** The major economic event was the Great Depression, which lasted most of the decade. Unemployment reached 13.7 million in the United States in 1932. Although men were considered the family's primary breadwinner when possible, women were also grateful for and sought out work.

1940s: During the war women entered the workforce but returned to homemaking when the war ended. They worked in factories and other places formerly identified with men in order to patriotically support the men who were overseas fighting.

Today: Many women work outside the home, even those with young children. They often do so in part because one salary can no longer adequately support a family. Another factor is the women's movement which has argued for equal treatment of men and women in politics and business and which has provided more diverse opportunities for women.

- **1930s and 1940s:** Works of literature could be easily censored when they were considered obscene, even if the material was subtle. Writers such as James Joyce and D. H. Lawrence often received a scandalized response from the general public.

  Today: Artistic merit and censorship remain an issue today. Although the works that were considered pornographic in the 1940s are frequently taught in high schools today, other works continue to be attacked. This is most evident when Congress considers the budget for the National Endowment for the Arts.

- **1930s and 1940s:** Romantic interactions between men and women were often formal and constrained. Men were expected to initiate dating situations and were also expected to introduce themselves to the woman's parents. A woman generally lived with her parents until she got married.

Today: Although some relationships are "conventional," the range of acceptable behavior between men and women is quite broad. Gender roles are no longer as rigid, although women still do the vast majority of housework and child care. In part because the age of marriage has risen, women as well as men often live independently before they get married, and couples frequently live together before they get married. Simultaneously, women can remain single if they choose without being considered "old maids."

Laura couldn't

- **1930s and 1940s:** Women seldom attended college or received any higher education. (Even for men, college was generally restricted to those who were financially comfortable.) If women attended a business school, they studied such subjects as typing and shorthand and prepared to be secretaries for bosses who would not have such skills.

  Today: The percentage of women and men attending college is nearly equal, although some fields, such as technology and engineering continue to be dominated by men. A person who aspires to work in an office, however, needs many more sophisticated skills. Shorthand, for example, is an outdated practice, and a person who can type is often not employable unless he or she also knows one or more computer programs.

The Boom Years

Another effect of returning soldiers was the passage of the G.I. Bill of Rights which provided education benefits and home loans for many veterans. As a result, college enrollment increased substantially and began to become more available to middle and lower class students. New home construction and suburban development also expanded. This meant that many middle-class people moved out of major cities. On the other hand, because of work available in factories, this decade also saw mass migration from rural areas into cities.

Technological innovations also occurred, although contemporary standards make them seem decidedly dated. In 1944, the first general-purpose digital computer began to operate at Harvard University—although it needed four seconds to perform multiplication problems and eleven seconds to perform division! This computer had been built with 760,000 parts and 500 miles of wire—clearly neither a desktop nor a laptop version. Although its inventors might not have anticipated the electronic age of the late twentieth century, they clearly initiated a technological revolution.

More pertinent to average Americans was the development of Kodacolor, a color film marketed by Eastman Kodak. This film permitted individuals to take color pictures with inexpensive cameras.

The Growth of Post-War Arts

Within the arts, Tennessee Williams worked in a rich context. Other plays performed in New York or major European cities included *The Searching Wind* by Lillian Hellman, *No Exit* by Jean-Paul Sartre, and *I Remember Mama* by John Van Druten, which included Marlon Brando in its cast. W. Somerset Maugham published his novel, *The Razor's Edge,* in 1944. Stephen Vincent Benet won the Pulitzer Prize for Poetry that year, and T. S. Eliot published his *Four Quartets*. Such well-known and talented painters as Pablo Picasso, Georgia O'Keeffe, and Frida Kahlo produced much of their work during this period. Cole Porter, Judy Garland, Rita Hay worth, and Gene Kelly were popular entertainers. On a more humorous note, 1944 also saw the introduction of the Chiquita Banana song, which encouraged consumers to identify the fruit with a particular brand name-a trend that reached mammoth proportions by the late twentieth century.

Critical Overview

When *The Glass Menagerie* reached the New York stage in 1945, it was a resounding success. A year earlier, it had also been successful in Chicago, despite poor weather which initially deterred the audience. According to Felicia Hardison Londre, writing in *American Playwrights since 1945,* "a crusade by the warmly enthusiastic Chicago critics" was launched to keep the play in production. It has remained popular, with staged as well as filmed versions appearing frequently, and it is considered to be one of Williams's most successful works. Indeed, writing in *The Christian Century* in 1964 while Williams was still alive, critic William R. Mueller stated that Williams "is the greatest living American playwright and ranks next to [Eugene] O'Neill in the history of American theater."

Critics almost inevitably remark on the poetic structure and language of *The Glass Menagerie.* As evidenced by the success with which his plays have been filmed, Williams brought a "cinematic concept of dramatic action to the American stage," according to Londre. She continued, describing Williams's work as characterized by "a harmonious blending and mutual reinforcement of dialogue, character, symbols, scenic environment, music, sound effects, and lighting." In his article Mueller stated that a "common denominator of Williams's plays is the quality of their poetry." Mueller defined this "poetry" not in terms of conventional poetic devices such as rhyme and meter, but as language "suffused with imagery and so phrased as to create a dreamlike state." In *Tennessee Williams: A Tribute,* S. Alan Chesler credited Williams with creating "a new poetic drama. . . . Williams has employed visual and auditory effects to previously unattempted extents by emphasizing color, music and scenic devices."

Yet poetry is far from the only characteristic for which critics have praised Williams and his plays. Although many of the stage directions in this play are almost novelistic in their detail, his work is also discussed in terms of its theatricality. Contrasting Williams with William Shakespeare, Mueller argued that "Shakespeare *can* be played without setting, lighting, costume, music; Williams cannot. He makes fullest use of the craft of the stage: scenic effects, lighting, color, music are of vast importance in evoking from the audience the desired emotional response." The use of a scrim between the audience and the actors at the beginning of the play would be one example of this. Another would be the frequency with which scene changes are signaled through fading music.

Critics also frequently comment on the psychological complexity of Williams's work, especially addressing the autobiographical roots of *The Glass Menagerie.* In part because of his success in creating characters who evoke empathy, even if they are not entirely typical, *The Glass Menagerie* and plays which soon followed appealed to an exceptionally broad audience, from high school students to professional critics. In the words of Foster Hirsch in *A Portrait of the Artist: The Plays of Tennessee Williams,* "Williams creates driven characters who are unlike anyone most of us are ever likely to meet and yet they are almost all convincing and recognizable." In an article published in *Players,* Gerald Berkowitz analyzed these characters in terms of the setting Williams has created for them: "as we discover each aberration or peculiarity in their [the Wingfields'] characters, we also discover that it is benign or even appropriate to their setting. Laura's pathological shyness does not stifle her at home; she is even able to overcome her fear of Jim when talking of her glass animals. Her lameness, which so embarrassed her in high school, becomes irrelevant when she is sitting in the apartment."

In addition to the number of awards Williams won during his lifetime, another way to measure his critical success, and the critical success of *The Glass Menagerie,* is through the professional attention he continues to receive. Books and articles continue to be written about this play as the thematic, literary, and theatrical issues it raises continue to be debated. Within the last generation, these publications include not only a wide range of American and Canadian periodicals but also journals published in Brussels, France, Brazil, The Netherlands, Germany, and South Africa. This play, in other words, has achieved not only significant popular success but international critical success.

Further Reading

Berkowitz, Gerald. "The 'Other World' of *The Glass Menagerie*" in *Players,* Vol. 48, no. 4, April-May, 1973, pp. 150-53.

> Berkowitz argues that the setting or "locus" of *The Glass Menagerie* as well as of other of Williams's plays influences perceptions of the characters to the extent that they seem "normal," while the "normal" people seem outsiders.

Burian, Jarka M. "The Glass Menagerie" in *International Dictionary of Theatre-1: Plays,* edited by Mark Hawkins-Dady, St. James Press, 1992, pp. 187-89.

> Burian provides several character analyses, focusing especially on Tom.

Chesler, S. Alan. "Tennessee Williams: Reassessment and Assessment" in *Tennessee Williams: A Tribute,* edited by Jac Tharpe, University Press of Mississippi, 1977, pp. 848-80.

> Chesler describes Williams's characteristics as a playwright and contextualizes his career in terms of his affect on American drama.

Hirsch, Foster. *A Portrait of the Artist: The Plays of Tennessee Williams,* Kennikat Press, 1979.

> Hirsch analyzes Williams's plays according to their autobiographical influences.

Londre, Felicia Hardison. "Tennessee Williams" in *American Playwrights since 1945: A Guide to Scholarship, Criticism, and Performance,* edited by Philip C. Kolin, Greenwood, 1989, pp. 488-517.

> Londre provides a thorough discussion of Williams's work and reputation, including a production history of several of his plays.

Moe, Christian H. "The Glass Menagerie" in *Reference Guide to American Literature,* edited by James Kamp, third edition, St. James Press, 1994.

> Moe traces the development of this play from a short story and describes the plot.

Mueller, William R. "Tennessee Williams: A New Direction?" in *The Christian Century,* Vol LXXXI, no. 42, October 14, 1964, pp. 1271-72.

> Mueller traces Williams's career, describing characteristics common to several plays. He suggests that Williams's earlier work was more successful, artistically, than his later plays.

Nelson, Benjamin. *Tennessee Williams: The Man and His Work,* Ivan Obolensky, 1961.

> Nelson critiques the body of Williams's work, evaluating the

plays in terms of each other.